CHALLENGE TO EUROPE: THE GROWING REFUGEE CRISIS

HEARING

BEFORE THE

SUBCOMMITTEE ON EUROPE, EURASIA, AND EMERGING THREATS

OF THE

COMMITTEE ON FOREIGN AFFAIRS HOUSE OF REPRESENTATIVES

ONE HUNDRED FOURTEENTH CONGRESS

FIRST SESSION

NOVEMBER 4, 2015

Serial No. 114–119

Printed for the use of the Committee on Foreign Affairs

Available via the World Wide Web: http://www.foreignaffairs.house.gov/ or
http://www.gpo.gov/fdsys/

U.S. GOVERNMENT PUBLISHING OFFICE

97–462PDF   WASHINGTON : 2015

For sale by the Superintendent of Documents, U.S. Government Publishing Office
Internet: bookstore.gpo.gov   Phone: toll free (866) 512–1800; DC area (202) 512–1800
Fax: (202) 512–2104   Mail: Stop IDCC, Washington, DC 20402–0001

CONTENTS

Page

WITNESSES

Gary Shiffman, Ph.D., adjunct professor, Center for Security Studies, George-
town University 4
V. Bradley Lewis, Ph.D., associate professor, School of Philosophy, The Catho-
lic University of America 13

LETTERS, STATEMENTS, ETC., SUBMITTED FOR THE HEARING

Gary Shiffman, Ph.D.: Prepared statement 7
V. Bradley Lewis, Ph.D.: Prepared statement 16

APPENDIX

Hearing notice 36
Hearing minutes 37

CHALLENGE TO EUROPE: THE GROWING REFUGEE CRISIS

WEDNESDAY, NOVEMBER 4, 2015

HOUSE OF REPRESENTATIVES,
SUBCOMMITTEE ON EUROPE, EURASIA, AND EMERGING THREATS,
COMMITTEE ON FOREIGN AFFAIRS,
Washington, DC.

The subcommittee met, pursuant to notice, at 3 o'clock p.m., in room 2200, Rayburn House Office Building, Hon. Dana Rohrabacher (chairman of the subcommittee) presiding.

Mr. ROHRABACHER. I call to order this hearing of the Europe, Eurasia, and Emerging Threats Subcommittee. As we begin today, I want to note that Congressman Meeks, the subcommittee's ranking member, is not with us today. He is recovering from a small, a minor, heart attack. We are grateful, very, very grateful, that it is a small one, and that he is on his way to recovery. He is on the mend, and we are looking forward to having him back with us very soon. I know I speak for all my colleagues, and we wish him the very, very best.

Turning the topic to this afternoon's hearing, I want to apologize for being late, but that is what happens when you have to do these hearings around votes.

The topic of this afternoon's hearing is a massive and increasing tide of asylum seekers, economic vibrance, stateless persons, and displaced people who have been and continue to enter Europe as we have seen, all seen, in the videos and news reports.

Migrants fleeing to Europe, they have been an issue of humanitarian concern for several years, but a wave of immigration erupted into a tsunami this summer, when the German Government announced it would ignore the Dublin rules and accept all Syrian refugees that made it to the German border. That announcement opened the gates for a flow of people to move from North Africa, the Middle East, and even Asia to transit through Greece, Turkey, the Balkans, and northward into Europe. With some notable exceptions, countries have simply facilitated the movement of migrants through their territory as quickly as possible, sometimes working to register the asylum seekers and sometimes not.

While individual stories of tragedy and humanitarian need are compelling, the aggregate number of people on the move is overwhelming. Earlier this week, the United Nations announced that 218,000 migrants crossed the Mediterranean Sea to Europe just last month. That is more than were recorded in all of 2014. It is expected that around 1 million asylum seekers of all origins will reach Germany in this year alone.

Germany and the EU are deeply divided about how to stem the flow of migrants, and what to do with those who have already entered. Clearly, what we have seen over the past few months is unsustainable, and if not checked, will change the fundamental nature of European countries, which are now being inundated.

What we are witnessing is the destruction of western civilization, not by an armed invasion, but instead, through envelopment. The effects of this will not soon disappear, but instead, could well turn out to be an historic change in the nature of many European countries.

Europe has been struggling to assimilate large Muslim populations, they have seen this in Europe. Increasing examples of anti-Semitism and radical Islamic violence clearly speak to the challenge of integration and the risk of failure in this situation. And that was before, of course, all of these—what we are talking about, these reports of this violence, and anti-Semitism, was before the current flow of immigrants began. Chancellor Merkel is full of confidence that Germany can educate, train, and turn refugees into productive and contributing members of society, but that is a tall task by any measure.

Even the most optimistic scenarios say that Europe will have to redirect billions and billions of dollars from supporting their own citizens, to accommodating the needs of these refugees.

I hope in our conversation today. We can examine and discuss, the massive influx of people into the Europe and what will be the consequences for European society, culture, and political institutions.

Without objection, all members will have 5 legislative days to submit additional written questions and extraneous materials for the record.

And I now will turn to Mr. Sires, who will give us his opening statement.

Mr. SIRES. Thank you, Mr. Chairman, for holding today's hearing on the migration and refugee crisis facing Europe, which many consider the worst migration and refugee crisis Europe has faced since World War II.

What is with the sound system?

Most of the migration is from refugees fleeing war-torn countries like Syria. The surge of migrants and refugees have significantly challenged and divided Europe, European countries, and the European Union. Many of the frontline states, such as Greece and Italy, find themselves overburdened with the influx of refugees and lack of sufficient resources to properly register and accommodate refugees and migrants.

It is clear that the EU and Europe, as a whole, must do a better job of coordinating efforts across its borders to manage the large number of people in a humane manner. As we work with our European partners to respond to the refugee crisis, we must remember the total influx of people our borders can cost. We have struggled with our own borders to absorb the surge of women and children fleeing violence in Central America. We have learned firsthand the importance of providing a response to these victims that is both timely and humane. Most importantly, these crises remind us that we can't lose sight of addressing the root causes of migration and finding a political solution to the war in Syria.

America has a long history of helping the world's most vulnerable people, and other countries look to the U.S. to lead when it comes to the refugees' resettlement. The administration recently announced that to accept 10,000 Syrian refugees, was the first sign of a goodwill to those that are desperate to flee the turmoil, but we can do much more.

In addition to increasing the number of refugees we accept on Syria, we can draw our own experience—to draw our own experiences and challenges regarding border security and provide assistance and increased coordination to our European allies to help them cope with the number of migrants and refugees.

I look toward to hearing from our esteemed panel of witnesses on the best path forward.

Thank you, Mr. Chairman, for holding the hearing.

Mr. ROHRABACHER. Does anyone else have an opening statement? Judge Poe.

Mr. POE. Thank you, Mr. Chairman.

Mr. Chairman, the crisis in Europe has resulted in thousands of refugees going to Europe, and not all of the people going into Europe are trying to escape the Syrian war. Now we understand there are people from all over the Middle East, even as far away as Afghanistan, and all fleeing, looking to move to Europe for various reasons. Not all of them are seeking asylum or refugee status, but may have other motives in mind as well.

I think part of the reason folks were moving so quick out of the Middle East and Syria is because Russia has gotten involved in Syria and is propping up Assad, trying to make sure he sticks around. And people see that their lives are in danger, so they leave the area.

Obviously, Europe was not prepared for this tremendous influx of thousands and thousands of other people. I am not sure that Europe has figured out a way to handle it, and I am sure the United States, in my opinion, is not doing much to help in the crisis. Some countries take various positions on what to do with the migrants, let them pass through or maybe not even let them come into their country. One such example is Hungary, who is trying to protect the national sovereignty of its own country. And the United States, rather than try to understand the situation in Hungary, even last week the U.S. Ambassador dressed down the Hungarians for what the State Department believed was not the right course in dealing with migrants. That does nothing to help our relationship with Hungary, a NATO ally.

It is obvious that there has to be something to be done with these thousands of individuals and where they are going and how long are they going to stay? And what is the United States going to do to help in this crisis? And I am sure that our witnesses have all the answers to these questions. That is why they are here. So I will thank the chairman, and I yield back.

Mr. ROHRABACHER. Mr. Weber, do you have an opening statement?

Mr. WEBER. We are good to go.

Mr. ROHRABACHER. Good to go?

Mr. WEBER. Yes.

Mr. ROHRABACHER. And I notice Ms. Frankel is as well.

Let me note that before we start, we have with us the distinguished Ambassador from Hungary. Thank you for joining us today. We appreciate that.

And let me just say that Hungary has been a tremendous friend and asset to the peace and stability of the world, and I am personally upset that our administration has sought to find out and try to complain about every little thing they disagree with, with Hungary. Hungary has every right to set their own policies, and I am pleased that Hungary has a track record of doing good things with the United States. So we thank you.

This is also the anniversary of the Hungarian revolution. And all of us who fought communism for decades were inspired by the young people and others who rose up against the communist dictatorship in Budapest back in 1956. So that is—is that 60 years?

Mr. POE. You were there.

Mr. ROHRABACHER. I was there. That was a little bit later.

But anyway, with that said, we have two really fine witnesses with us today. I would ask if you could try to get it to 5 minutes, and then we will have a nice dialogue on that.

I would like to introduce Dr. Gary Shiffman. He is a professor of security studies, Department of Georgetown University. His work focuses on exploring the relationship between economics and national security. Dr. Shiffman is also the founder of Giant Oak Incorporated, a company that meets the demand for social science-driven innovation in big data environments like institutions countering organized crime, money laundering, trafficking, insurgency, and terrorism. It is a pleasure to have Dr. Shiffman here to speak with us on this very important topic.

Also, we have with us Dr. V. Bradley Lewis. He serves as associate professor in the School of Philosophy at Catholic University of America, where he has taught for nearly two decades. He also serves as associate editor of the American Journal of Jurisprudence. Dr. Lewis specializes in political philosophy, Plato, legal philosophy, and natural law theory. We are delighted to have Dr. Lewis with us today.

And, again, I ask if Dr. Lewis and Dr. Shiffman could keep it to about 5 minutes, and we will have a nice dialogue. So thank you very much.

Dr. Shiffman, Gary, you may go first.

STATEMENT OF GARY SHIFFMAN, PH.D, ADJUNCT PROFESSOR, CENTER FOR SECURITY STUDIES, GEORGETOWN UNIVERSITY

Mr. SHIFFMAN. Thank you, distinguished members of the subcommittee, for inviting me to provide testimony today on the economic views of security implications of the security——

Mr. ROHRABACHER. You have to push the button.

Mr. SHIFFMAN. Okay. Is that better? There we go.

I can offer two distinct perspectives on this challenge. First, as a behavioral scientist and as a former senior official at U.S. Customs and Border Protections, I have spent a lot of time thinking about how understanding essential characteristics of human behavior can inform our understanding of organized violence.

I have divided my comments today into three sections. The first provides an economist's view of a way to think about security and the refugees. The second discusses my experience as a practitioner of national and Homeland Security. And third suggests a framework for policy options.

One, a behavioral economist's perspective. Economists see all human interactions as exchanges taking place within markets, with individuals regardless of race, religion, or ethnicity, making decisions that maximize welfare for ourselves, our families, and our communities. Competitive marketplaces demand cooperation in order to maximize our goals, leading individuals to divide the world into us and them. Political violence, such as insurgency and terrorism, occurs when scarce conditions allow violence to become economically feasible. In other words, people choose violence when it is the best way to achieve their goals in the face of scarce resources.

In Europe today, continuing mass refugee streams will continue to strain resources of European populations, creating conditions of scarcity that highlight competition and sharpen divides between host and refugee, between us and them.

As we may have predicted, we are witnessing political parties and viewing rhetoric with divisive language manipulating us versus them narratives and exacerbating tensions. This increasingly divisive rhetoric recalls historical examples of politicians using hate-creating stories to discredit opponents and better their own positions. Harvard economist, Edward Glaeser, points to three examples: Anti-Black hatred in the American South, anti-Semitism in Europe, and anti-Americanism in the Arab world. These hateful narratives lead Glaeser to point out that when populations are socially isolated and politically relevant, stories of hatred are likely to take hold and recruitment and violence can follow.

European States and the EU stand at a crossroads between becoming a melting pot or remaining a federation of nations with distinct national ethnic and religious identities. The economists view would suggest that regardless of the choice, policies that create politically relevant and socially isolated populations be avoided. So how do we do this? Section 2, reflections of the practitioner.

Regarding security challenges, we focus on two primary vectors. First, the possibility for terrorists to embed themselves within refugee streams and the potential for radicalization among refugee communities. High levels of single men in the refugee populations raises concerns that extremist groups, such as ISIL, have embedded members in the refugee streams. Existing radicalization of European societies coupled with the widening gulf between host and guest communities raises real concerns on the potential for refugees to radicalize and become violent.

With regard to border security, the United States offers an opportunity for comparison. The United States screens for terrorist risk factors throughout the screening and asylum processes. The United States does a good job of integrating immigrants and refugees when they arrive, and significantly, the United States does not require border states to take full responsibility for border security costs. Instead, the bulk of the responsibility is shared across the entire tax base of all States. This poses a comparative question: Is the European Union, as a collective, capable of sharing the costs and the benefits of screening and integration? To what extent should border states such as Hungary and Slovenia bear the brunt of this responsibility?

Section 3, some thoughts on the response framework. The European Union is capable of benefiting from the refugee streams if it approaches the refugees as a source of needed workers while managing risk. Despite this potential benefit, EU member states may not have the capacity to address the speed and scale of the current flows either from a fiscal or a security standpoint, especially in the border states where the initial asylum claims are made.

Issues of preserving national identity are real and must be treated as legitimate policy goals. As a result, governments will need to choose who is permitted to enter Europe by increasing screening measures limiting entry and sharing the fiscal responsibilities. Screening measures might be improved through cooperation and data analysis. Limiting entry might focus either on the most vulnerable population, such as women and children, or on populations fleeing from ISIL-controlled areas. And in integrating refugee populations into the labor force might mitigate fears of radicalization by avoiding isolation and minimizing social welfare costs.

So my three key takeaways, first, regardless of the decision made on numbers and locations of refugee flows, threats may emanate from socially isolated and politically relevant populations.

Two, the EU can manage risks associated with terrorism and other organized violence, but perhaps not each member state possesses the capacities, so we need to think about shared costs and benefits.

And three, the EU is capable of benefiting from the refugee streams if it approaches the problem as an opportunity to integrate a needed workforce. Thank you.

Mr. ROHRABACHER. Mr. Lewis.

[The prepared statement of Mr. Shiffman follows:]

Gary M. Shiffman, Ph.D.
Georgetown University [1]
Giant Oak, Inc.

House Committee on Foreign Affairs

"An Economist's View of the Security Implications of the Refugee Crisis in Europe"
Challenge to Europe: The Growing Refugee Crisis

Before the Subcommittee on Europe, Eurasia, and Emerging Threats
United States House of Representatives

November 4, 2015

Distinguished members of the Subcommittee on Europe, Eurasia, and Emerging Threats, thank you for inviting me to provide testimony on an economic view of the security implications of the refugee crisis in Europe.

I can offer two distinct perspectives on this challenge to the committee today. As a behavioral scientist and as a former senior official at U.S. Customs and Border Protection, I have spent a lot of time thinking about how understanding essential characteristics of human behavior can inform our understanding of organized violence and thereby promote security.

I have divided my comments into three sections: the first provides an economist's view of a way to think about security and the refugees; the second discusses my experience as a practitioner of national and homeland security; and the third suggests a framework for committee members to consider when hearing testimony in future hearings on policy options.

I. A Behavioral Economist's Perspective of the Refugee Crisis

Economists see all human interaction as exchanges taking place within markets, with individuals – regardless of race, religion, or ethnicity – making decisions that maximize benefit and welfare for ourselves, our families, and our communities. Competitive marketplaces demand cooperation in order to maximize our goals, leading individuals to divide the world into 'us' and 'them' on the basis of perceived or actual kinship. Political violence such as insurgency and terrorism occurs when scarce conditions allow violence to become economically feasible. In other words, people choose violence when it is the best way to achieve their goals in the face of scarce resources.

Applying this Perspective to Europe:

In Europe today, continuing mass refugee streams will continue to strain resources of European states and populations, creating conditions of scarcity that highlight competition and sharpen divides between host and refugee—between "us" and "them"—communities.

As we may have predicted, we have witnessed political parties imbuing their rhetoric with divisive language, manipulating the 'us vs. them' narrative and exacerbating tensions:

- The Budapest Times recently published an OpEd comparing the migrant populations to a Trojan Horse full of "unwanted Muslims" and possible terrorists aiming to conquer Europe; [2]
- Germany's increasing political violence associated with the refugee crisis, including the recent stabbing of a senior official responsible for welfare in Cologne, has sparked debates on censoring hate speech on social media. [3]

This increasingly divisive rhetoric recalls historical examples of politicians using "hate-creating stories" to discredit opponents and better their own positions. For example, Harvard economist Edward Glaeser points to three examples: Anti-Black hatred in the American South; Anti-Semitism in Europe; and Anti-Americanism in the Arab World.[4]

- Following the American Civil War, changes in the political landscape and redistributive policies led to hateful narratives portraying Blacks as dangerous to Whites, exacerbating racial tensions;
- Late 19th-century right-wing politicians in Germany, Austria, and Russia used anti-Semitic language to discredit Jewish leftist politicians and left-wing policies that would redistribute wealth; and
- Anti-American narratives in the Arab and Islamic worlds point to Western colonial actions and more recent U.S. support to Israel to justify political violence.

These hateful narratives led Glaser to point out that when populations are socially isolated but politically relevant, stories of hatred are likely to take hold. *And recruitment and violence can follow.* These stories, although not based in fact, can allow for political movements to avoid wealth-redistributing policies.

European states and the EU stand at a crossroads between becoming a melting pot or remaining a federation of nations with distinct national, ethnic, and religious identities. The economist's view would suggest that, regardless of the choice, policies that create politically relevant and socially isolated populations be avoided.

How would we do this?

II. Reflections as a Practitioner of National and Homeland Security

If one were to choose to prevent some or all refugees from crossing a border, we know how to do this. We obtain operational control of borders through the effective application of three resources: people, technology, and infrastructure. We apply these three resources optimally, depending on factors such as terrain and population characteristics such as density and diversity.

Although we know how to control borders, implementing these controls poses serious fiscal challenges to the government. We know this well in the United States. Applying this perspective to Europe, it seems that the response to Europe's refugee crisis must be collectively shared.

Regarding security challenges, concern primarily focuses on two vectors: the possibility for terrorists to embed within refugee streams, and the potential radicalization among refugee communities.

The high levels of single men in the refugee populations raises concerns that extremist groups such as ISIL have embedded members in the refugee streams. Asylum records state that nearly 70% of migrants and refugees are men, frequently seeking opportunities abroad to send money back to their families who remained in conflict zones.[5]

However, terrorism expert Dan Byman has pointed to ISIL's operational focus on drawing Muslims to the conflict, rather than pushing them away, and the lack of empirical evidence that terrorists use refugee streams as bases of operation, provide indication that these fears are currently only speculative.[6]

Existing radicalization in European societies, coupled with the widening gulf between host and guest communities, raises real concerns on the potential for refugees to radicalize and become violent. Violence does not stem from the marginalization itself, but rather marginalization creates opportunities that facilitate the entrepreneurs of organized violence. Think of recruitment.

With regard to border security, the United States offers a comparative approach to the European stance.

- The United States screens for terrorist risk factors throughout the screening and asylum processes at our borders.
- The United States does a good job of integrating immigrants and refugees.
- And significantly, the United States does not require border states such as California, Arizona, New Mexico, and Texas to take full responsibility for border security costs. Instead, the bulk of the responsibility is shared across the tax base of all states.

This poses the comparative question: is the European Union as a collective capable of sharing both benefits and costs of screening and integration? To what extent should border states, such as Hungary and Slovenia, bear the brunt of this responsibility alone?

III. Some Thoughts on a Response Framework

The European Union is capable of benefiting from the refugee streams if it approaches the refugees as a source of needed workers *while managing risks*.

Despite this potential benefit, EU member states may not have the capacity to address the speed and scale of the current refugee flows from either a fiscal or security standpoint, especially in the border states where initial asylum claims are made.

Issues of preserving national identity are real and must be treated as legitimate policy goals. As a result, governments will need to choose who is permitted to enter Europe by increasing screening measures, limiting entry, and sharing the fiscal responsibilities.

- Screening measures might include: expanding background checks, improving international communication and data sharing; and focusing intelligence resources on migrant populations;[7]
- Limiting entry might focus either on the most vulnerable populations, such as women and children, or on populations fleeing the United States' and Europe's primary adversaries, such as ISIL-controlled areas;

- Integrating refugee populations into the labor force might mitigate fears of radicalization by avoiding isolation and minimizing social welfare costs.

The majority of migrants and refugees are neither impoverished, nor uneducated, as they are the individuals who can afford to pay smugglers to cross the border. Capitalizing on existing skill sets and providing legitimate work opportunities might reduce the opportunities for violent entrepreneurs to take advantage of economic marginalization.

Additionally, it will be necessary to avoid perceptions of unfair political advantage in order to lessen the divide between refugee and host communities. Political rhetoric vilifying refugee populations builds on the perception that refugees strain host country resources. Providing work opportunities and assistance to migrant populations may further exacerbate these tensions by appearing to favor 'the other,' increasing competition for jobs, housing, and resources. Combatting this rhetoric and implementing programming to build resiliency between host and refugee communities will be essential to successful integration.

Key Takeaways and Conclusion

1. Regardless of the decisions made on numbers and locations of refugee flows, threats may emanate from socially isolated and politically relevant populations.
2. The EU can manage risks associated with terrorism and other organized violence, but perhaps not each member state possess these capacities, so we need to think about shared costs and shared benefits.
3. The EU is capable of benefiting from the refugee streams if it approaches the problem as an opportunity to integrate a needed work force.

Thank You.

---

[1] Gary M. Shiffman is an adjunct professor at Georgetown University and President and CEO of Giant Oak, Inc. A team of Georgetown University Security Studies graduate students (Gary Anthony, Joshua Forgét, Mia Ramesh, and Kathleen Walsh) contributed research for this testimony.
[2] George F. Hemingway, "Migrants or Conquistadors, the New Europeans.'" *The Budapest Times*. October 25, 2015.
[3] Allison Smale, "Anti-Immigrant Violence in Germany Spurs New Debate on Hate Speech," *The New York Times*. October 21, 2015.

[4] Edward L. Glaeser, "The Political Economy of Hatred," *The Quarterly Journal of Economics*. 120 (1). 2005.

[5] "Asylum Statistics," *Eurostat*. May 21, 2015. <http://ec.europa.eu/eurostat/statistics-explained/index.php/Asylum_statistics>

[6] Daniel Byman, "Do Syrian Refugees Pose a Terrorism Threat?" *The Brookings Institution*. October 27, 2015.

[7] Seth Jones, "Testimony before the House Homeland Security Committee, Subcommittee on Counterterrorism and Intelligence: The Terrorism Threat to the United States and Implications for Refugees," *RAND*. June 24, 2015.

13

STATEMENT OF V. BRADLEY LEWIS, PH.D., ASSOCIATE PROFESSOR, SCHOOL OF PHILOSOPHY, THE CATHOLIC UNIVERSITY OF AMERICA

Mr. LEWIS. Thank you. Chairman Rohrabacher, and members of the subcommittee. It isn't often that a political philosopher is invited to speak to a congressional committee, and I am honored by your invitation.

I have been asked to speak about the present migration crisis in Europe from the perspective of political philosophy. Much of what we need to know about the migration crisis is simply empirical. How many persons are involved? Where are they from? Why are they migrating? Et cetera. Philosophy has little to say about these questions. Rather, political philosophy is the business of understanding what principles or reasons should guide our political conduct and shape our institutions and laws; what are the starting points for our thinking about our actions as persons and communities? Our starting points are actual goods that direct all of our practical reasoning. Political philosophy must also be attentive to truths about how human beings characteristically behave; that is, about the stable aspects of human nature.

Political communities provide a context for individuals and groups to pursue their own development. This context includes especially legal systems that authoritatively coordinate the actions and interactions of persons and groups. Political communities are required by and justified by the common good of the people who constitute them. By common good I mean, first, the integral development and flourishing of the persons who live in the community and, secondly, the whole ensemble of conditions that facilitate that development. It is these things that justify but also limit the exercise of political authority.

Among the conditions required for persons in groups to thrive, are the availability of resources, and these resources first come from the earth itself. And no things, no products from the earth, no parts of it, naturally and originally, belong to any particular persons; however, human nature suggests that those things are best maintained when they are shared out in some distribution of private property.

And I believe that this explanation of private property is also the sound reason for the existence of different territorial political communities. Governments and their constituents together are analogous to property owners in the sense that they represent a determinate agency responsible for the maintenance of the necessary conditions in a recognized territory or jurisdiction, justified by the directedness of the agency and those conditions to the common good of their people.

Public order, the security of persons, both individuals and groups and their property and freedom, are essential elements of the common good and are best protected by particular governments with clear jurisdictions. The common good is more than merely a set of laws and institutions. It includes a common culture, among the elements of which are, for example, a common language, at least one common language, and shared sentiments of attachment and common membership. Such sentiments are an indispensable support for the maintenance of legal and political institutions and make possible the sacrifices that are necessary for the preservation of any political community over time. This is especially the case with respect to modern democracies, which tend to be large and which often encompass considerable diversity of ethnicity, religious faith, and moral views among their populations, in addition to the social mobility and dynamism characteristic of modern economies.

The role of shared practices, values, and sentiments in the maintenance of stable political communities that really do promote the common good of their citizens was known to Plato and Aristotle at the very beginning of the tradition. Aristotle in particular elaborated the notion of political friendship based on a fundamental agreement, or like-mindedness, about the purpose, structure, and practices of the political system.

In the 19th Century, Alexis de Tocqueville famously made the habits and mores of the people central to his accounts of how democratic political institutions were maintained in the United States.

The willingness of citizens not only to defend one another through military service, but also to consent in the sort of redistributive taxation common to contemporary welfare states assumes a sense of common membership and shared values and sentiments. Without these things, the maintenance of communities and their institutions would require the application of coercive force on a far greater scale than we associate with free societies.

Similarly, among these supports for free governments, are more generic but nevertheless, dearly bought values like the rule of law, an atmosphere in which legal and natural rights of persons are acknowledged and protected by the law with habits of civility and mutual forbearance that are informed by civic and political friendship.

The common good of the political community is challenged, if not threatened, by the sudden and disorderly influx of large numbers of foreigners. And so the very common good that justifies political authority also justifies, I would say requires, government's concern about who enters their territory, and even more importantly, about the assimilation of immigrants into the community. Both the need to protect public order and the need to assimilate, justify concern about the number of immigrants into the country and their character.

A large group of immigrants who come predominantly from a distinct region of the world with its own culture that is significantly different from that of their country of destination presents an obvious challenge that no government could responsibly ignore. Indeed, there may be particularly urgent concerns if the immigrant group contains large numbers of persons who are from places where genuine political community has not emerged and more social life is still dominated by family and tribal loyalties, or who are reasonably believed to hold views that are inconsistent with democratic political institutions and the protection of basic human rights, especially the equal legal rights of women and religious freedom.

Large numbers hastily or heedlessly admitted cannot only strain a country's material infrastructure of social support, but its legal system and larger political culture. Moreover, it could set in motion changes, the full import of which may not be immediately apparent but which could lead to various forms of social and political instability later.

The collision we witness today in Europe of immense numbers of immigrants from a distinct civilization with a demographic collapse of Western European countries, countries with birth rates well below replacement levels, cannot but have far-reaching consequences not only for the internal politics of those countries, but also for the neighboring countries of Central and Eastern Europe and at some stage for the United States as well. Since we cannot now know what kind of political pressure may eventually brought to bear on those countries' governments relative to the character and future of the Western alliance. Thank you.

Mr. ROHRABACHER. Well, thank you very much.

[The prepared statement of Mr. Lewis follows:]

Written Statement of V. Bradley Lewis, Ph.D.
Associate Professor, School of Philosophy
The Catholic University of America
House Committee on Foreign Affairs
Subcommittee on Europe, Eurasia, and Emerging Threats
Hearing: Challenge to Europe: The Growing Migration Crisis
4 November 2015

Chairman Rohrabacher, Ranking Member Meeks, Members of the Subcommittee: It isn't often that a political philosopher is invited to speak to a congressional committee, and I am honored by your invitation. I have been asked to talk about the migration crisis in Europe from the perspective of political philosophy, and I want to do that by making three points. First, I want to say just a bit about what political philosophy has to contribute to our understanding of this sort of issue. Second, I want to sketch out some of the elements of the tradition of classical political philosophy that are relevant to the question, as well as some recent applications of that tradition. Third, and on the basis of my sketch, I also want to suggest what the nature of the migration crisis is beyond its obvious and compelling humanitarian dimension, and why it is one that we cannot responsibly ignore. My view of the matter is informed by principles that can be somewhat peremptorily stated in three theses: first, government exists and legitimately exercises its authority over a territory and its people in order to secure and promote their common good; second, that good includes institutions and laws, but also a culture made up of habits, sentiments, and values shared by the people that provide indispensable support for those laws and institutions; and third, the people and their government have a legitimate interest in who enters their territory, in prudently regulating immigration, and in effecting the assimilation of immigrants into their own culture and institutions. Indeed, governments have an obligation to do these things, one that certainly requires a careful balance of generosity and the just regard for the well-being of their own communities.

1. Political Philosophy and Practical (Political) Reasoning

Much of what we need to know about the migration crisis is simply empirical: how many persons are involved? Where are they from? Why are they migrating? What do they hope to receive? What might they contribute? What material capacities do the receiving countries have to receive them and what are the limits of those material capacities? Philosophy has little to say about these questions. Rather, political philosophy is the business of understanding what principles or reasons should guide our political conduct and shape our institutions and laws. What are the starting points for our thinking about our actions as persons and communities? Our starting points are the actual goods that direct all of our practical reasoning. Political philosophy must also be attentive to truths about how human beings characteristically behave, that is, about the stable aspects of human nature. This sort of practical reasoning must here be deployed particularly in the deliberation of European governments and the people they represent in determining how many migrants to accept and on what conditions. It also involves evaluation of the claims of migrants themselves to freely cross borders and remain in host countries, and correlatively, the right of those countries to deny entry. Do people have a right to move freely across national boundaries and are there legitimate limitations on such a right? This leads back to more abstract questions about the reasons governments can be said to legitimately exist in the first place and what their legitimate powers are with respect to the persons who may wish to enter their national territory.

These rather abstract observations point out two crucial facts about political communities: they do claim to exercise authority (and not just force), and such claims generally assume jurisdiction that is territorial. Political philosophy has had rather little to say about some of these questions, e.g., what justifies the coming into being of particular states in particular places and what principled connections exist between territorial jurisdictions and cultural identities existing among the persons who inhabit such territories? Recent political philosophy in particular has tended towards the construction of highly abstract accounts of the sorts of principles that should regulate the distribution of wealth and resources and the character of public debate about individual rights and constitutional structures. The more elemental questions about states and their identity, however, have not been adequately developed.

2. Political Authority, the Common Good, and Borders

My second point, however, is to suggest that the tradition of classical western political philosophy can help here. I will state a few theses fairly dogmatically: first, human beings are such that they cannot achieve their full and integrated development alone. At a minimum we need the love and care of parents, but beyond that, the most distinctive forms of human happiness or flourishing require us to cooperate with one another at different levels. Throughout history persons have associated with one another in families, clans or other groups based on extended familial relationships, and, ultimately, political community. Political communities are, as Aristotle first noted, distinctive in two crucial respects: first, they have a kind of completeness, that is, they encompass all the other human associations and provide within themselves all of the goods needed for integral human flourishing. Second, genuinely political communities are communities of reason.[1] This does not mean they are "rationalistic" in a narrow sense; it means rather that they are communities in which public decisions are made by processes of rational deliberation among the people themselves and their elected representatives and not simply on the basis of kinship. Genuine *political* community thus transcends (without destroying) family and tribal identity because those sub-political groups cannot provide all that we need and because they do not operate in themselves on the basis of reason.

Second, complete political communities thus provide a context for individuals and groups to pursue their own development; this context includes especially legal systems that authoritatively coordinate the actions and interactions of persons and groups. Political communities are required by and justified by the common good of the people who constitute them. By common good I mean first, the integral development and flourishing of all of the persons who live in the community, and second, the whole ensemble of conditions that facilitate that development.[2] It is these things that justify, but also limit the exercise of political authority. The common good in this sense is not and cannot be opposed to the goods of the persons who make up the community. Its commonness is not that of a kind of super-individual over and against the natural persons who make up the community; rather, it is a good that is common because it is a good *for all of those persons*. Aristotle distinguished between true political systems and those he regarded as corrupt precisely by reference to whether they served the common good of the community or only the good of the ruler or ruling class.[3] This distinction has ever since been the ground of distinguishing between free or constitutional government and tyranny and was expressed

---

[1] Aristotle *Nicomachean Ethics*, bk. 1, ch. 1, at 1094a25-b10; *Politics*, bk. 1, ch. 2, at 1252b30-1253a18.

[2] See John Finnis, *Natural Law and Natural Rights*, 2d ed. (Oxford: Oxford University Press, 2011), 147-56.

[3] Aristotle *Politics*, bk. 3, ch. 7, at 1279a22-b11. See also Plato *Laws* 712d-715b, 875a-d; Xenophon *Hiero* 11.1; Cicero *Republic* 1.25, 33, 3.31; Thomas Aquinas, *On Kingship*, 1.2-3; *Summa theologiae*, 1-2, 95.4c, 96.4c, 105.1c.

memorably in our Declaration of Independence's affirmation that "Governments are instituted among men" in order "to secure" the "unalienable rights" of "life, liberty, and the pursuit of happiness" by men who were "self-evident[ly] . . . created equal."[4] The common good of the community, therefore, is the end and purpose of political institutions and those institutions themselves (and all that supports and animates them) are a common good of the people.

Third, among the conditions required for individual persons and groups to thrive are the availability of resources, which first come to us from the earth itself: the land is the first and ultimate source of food, clothing, shelter, and every other good useful for human life. The earth and its resources belong originally to no one in particular: no part of it is *naturally* the property of any particular person. Human beings, however, must appropriate and use things in order to live and develop, so some scheme of distribution must be adopted. Again, Aristotle was the first philosopher to see that this distribution was crucially conditioned by human nature itself: we tend not to take the best care of things we do not own; when too many people are in charge of the maintenance of something, confusion and neglect often follow; and when one useful good is given to many, quarrelling and conflict are often the result. For all these reasons the private ownership of property makes the most sense, provided that ownership is exercised with a view to the common good.[5] I believe that this explanation of private property is also the sound reason for the existence of different territorial political communities.[6] Governments and their constituents together are analogous to property owners in the sense that they represent a determinate agency responsible for the maintenance of the necessary conditions in a recognized territory (jurisdiction) justified by the directedness of that agency and those conditions to the common good of the people. Public order, the security of persons—both individuals and groups—and their property and freedom, are essential elements of the common good and are best protected by particular governments with clear jurisdiction. Territorial boundaries are essential (certainly in the modern world) to the effective jurisdiction of governments in their making and enforcing of the laws that protect and promote the common good of the community. They are also essential to assigning and evaluating accountability for the maintenance of the common good, for knowing whom to blame when the people's business is poorly done or not done at all.

3. Political Culture and the Nature of the Migration Crisis

My third point expands and connects these theses to the present European migration crisis. The common good is more than simply laws and institutions. Indeed, for Aristotle the laws follow a city's constitutional order or regime (*politeia*), which Aristotle defined both as the order of its ruling offices, but also as its "way of life."[7] It is the regime that determines the kind of laws[8] a city has as well as what

---

[4] Declaration of Independence (4 July 1776), ¶2. Cf. Abraham Lincoln, First Inaugural Address (4 March 1861), in *The Collected Works of Abraham Lincoln*, ed. Roy P. Basler (New Brunswick, NJ: Rutgers University Press, 1953) 4: 269 with the Gettysburg Address (19 November 1864) in ibid., 7: 21 ("government of the people, by the people, and for the people") with discussion in Jacques Maritain, *Man and the State* (Chicago: University of Chicago Press, 1951), 9-27.

[5] See Aristotle *Politics*, bk. 2, ch. 5; Thomas Aquinas, *Summa theologiae*, 2-2, 66.2c.

[6] See the brief but important discussion in John Finnis, "Law, Universality, and Social Identity," in Finnis, *Intention and Identity* (Oxford: Oxford University Press, 2011), 120; and "Cosmopolis, Nation States and Families," in ibid., 125; and "Migration Rights," in Finnis, *Human Rights and Common Good* (Oxford: Oxford University Press, 2011), 120. A similar suggestion was made by John Rawls, *The Law of Peoples* (Cambridge, MA: Harvard University Press, 1999), 38-39.

[7] Aristotle *Politics*, bk. 3, ch. 6, at 1278b8-10; book 4, ch. 10, at 1295a40-b1.

we might call its ethos or, in a more contemporary idiom, its "culture."[9] Modern states are, of course, far larger and more internally complex than the city-states of Aristotle's day. Nevertheless, the basic point endures: a political community is more than simply its laws and administrative structures. It includes a common culture, among the elements of which are, for example, a common language (at least one) and shared sentiments of attachment and common membership. We often associate these things with a reality that transcends laws and institutions both immediately and over time often referred to as the "nation." Where laws and institutions are simply constructed, nations are not; they develop over time and not according to any predetermined plan.[10] It is to the nation that patriotism attaches, and while patriotism may be related to laws and institutions, it includes many other sentiments and is directed to (integrally) the way of life of *this* people in *this* place and expresses a gratitude for the fact that so much of one's own access to the goods that allow us to flourish are conditioned by their instantiation in and protection by *this* community.

Such sentiments are an indispensable support for the maintenance of legal and political institutions and make possible the sacrifices that are necessary for the preservation of any political community over time. This is especially the case with respect to modern democracies, which tend to be large and which often encompass considerable diversity of ethnicities, religious faiths, and even moral views in their populations, in addition to the social mobility and dynamism characteristic of modern economies.[11] The role of shared practices, values, and sentiments in the maintenance of stable political communities that really do promote the common good of their citizens was known to Plato and Aristotle at the very beginning of the tradition. Aristotle, in particular, elaborated a notion of political friendship, based on a fundamental agreement or like-mindedness (*homonoia*) about the purpose, structure, and practices of the political system.[12] In the nineteenth century Alexis de Tocqueville famously made the habits and mores of the people central to his account of how democratic political institutions were maintained in the US.[13] This link between the endurance of democratic institutions and political culture, including some sense of national identity, has been frequently repeated by contemporary political theorists as well on the basis of both philosophical principles and empirical data.[14] The willingness of citizens not only to defend one another through military service, but also to consent in the sort of redistributive taxation common to contemporary welfare states assumes a sense of common membership and shared

---

[8] Aristotle *Politics*, bk. 4, ch. 1, at 1289a13-15.

[9] See Leo Strauss, Natural Right and History (Chicago: University of Chicago Press, 1953), 136-37; Stephen G. Salkever, *Finding the Mean: Theory and Practice in Aristotelian Political Philosophy* (Princeton, NJ: Princeton University Press, 1990), 81-88.

[10] See Maritain, *Man and the State*, 4-9.

[11] For a fairly moderate statement of this view see David Miller, *On Nationality* (Oxford: Oxford University Press, 1995).

[12] See especially Aristotle *Nicomachean Ethics*, bk. 8, ch. 9, and bk. 9, ch. 6; as well as Plato *Laws* 627e-628a, 693b, 694b, 701d, 738d-e, 759b, 771d-e, and especially 793b-d..

[13] Alexis de Tocqueville, *Democracy in America* (1830-35), trans. Harvey C. Mansfield and Delba Winthrop (Chicago: University of Chicago Press, 2000), 274-302, 407-410. In his emphasis on habits and mores, Tocqueville was likely influenced by Jean-Jacques Rousseau, who held that the mores, customs, and opinions of citizens were more important than any of the laws: see *On the Social Contract* (1791), bk. 3, ch. 12.

[14] Consider, e.g., Pierre Manent, *A World Beyond Politics? A Defense of the Nation-State*, trans. Marc LePain (Princeton, NJ: Princeton University Press, 2006), 51-69; *Democracy Without Nations?*, trans. Paul Seaton (Wilmington, DE: ISI Books, 2007); and Larry Diamond, *The Spirit of Democracy* (New York: Times Books, 2008), 153-68.

values and sentiments. Without these things the maintenance of communities and their institutions would require the application of coercive force on a far greater scale than we associate with free societies.[15]

Similarly among these supports for free government are more generic (or universal), but nevertheless dearly bought, values like the Rule of Law, a widespread commitment to the equal treatment of persons who live in the state of ordered liberty made possible by a system of laws that are typically prospective and not retroactive, possible to comply with, clearly promulgated, coherent with one another, stable enough to allow one to plan one's own actions legally, and administered consistently by officials who are accountable for their action or inaction.[16] This too is a crucial element of the common good as is an atmosphere in which the legal and natural rights of persons are acknowledged and protected by law, and in which political debate and competition are grounded in rational argument and carried out according to habits of civility and mutual forbearance, informed by the sort of civic or political friendship mentioned above.[17] Such practices are possible where the relationship of citizens is informed by an ethic of reciprocity born of a sense of membership, a kind of political trust, and the recognition not only of a common past, but commitment to a common future for *this* people.

It should go without saying that the sort of political culture I have attempted to describe is not racial. Racial and ethnic diversity do not in themselves pose problems for stable political communities where the elements of the common good I have described exist and are accepted. There is also no reason why regular, orderly immigration into a political community is inconsistent with its common good. What is important is that newcomers are properly assimilated, that they come to share the values and sentiments of the community that are necessary to support its laws and institutions, as well as the more generic values like the rule of law, the protection of human rights, and the practice of orderly and rational self-government. This process is itself an aspect of the common good of a community and is therefore accordingly an appropriate matter for regulation by the legitimate governing authority. Among the reasonable tasks of such an authority is the distribution of membership in the community and the establishment of reasonable conditions for membership as well as specific decisions about when and to whom membership is granted.[18]

The common good of a political community *is* challenged, if not threatened, by the sudden and disorderly influx of large numbers of foreigners, and so the very common good that justifies political authority itself also justifies—I would say requires—governments' concern about who enters their territory and, even more importantly, about the assimilation of immigrants into the community. Both the need to protect public order and the need to assimilate justify concern about the number of immigrants into a country and their character. A large group of immigrants who come predominantly from a distinct region with its own culture that is significantly different from that of their country of destination presents an obvious challenge that no government could responsibly ignore. Indeed, there may be particularly urgent concerns if the immigrant group contains large numbers of persons who are

---

[15] See the discussion in Joseph Raz, "Multiculturalism," *Ratio Juris* 11 (1998): 202, and Finnis, "Law, Universality, and Social Identity," 114-19.

[16] See Lon L. Fuller, *The Morality of Law*, rev. ed. (New Haven: Yale University Press, 1969), ch. 2.

[17] For a powerful statement of the point with specific application to the question of immigration see Thomas Jefferson, *Notes on the State of Virginia*, in *The Life and Selected Writings of Thomas Jefferson*, ed. Adrienne Koch and William Peden (New York: The Modern Library, 1993), 204.

[18] See Michael Walzer, *Spheres of Justice: A Defense of Pluralism and Equality* (New York: Basic Books, 1983), ch. 2.

from places where genuinely *political* community has not emerged and where social life is still dominated by family and tribal loyalties or who are reasonably believed to hold views that are inconsistent with democratic political institutions and the protection of basic human rights, especially the equal legal rights of women and religious freedom. Large numbers hastily or heedlessly admitted can not only strain a country's material infrastructure of social support, but its legal system, and larger political culture. Moreover, it could set in motion changes the full import of which may not be immediately apparent, but which could lead to various forms of social and political instability later.

The collision we witness today in Europe of immense numbers of immigrants from a distinct civilization with the demographic collapse of Western European countries, countries with birthrates well below replacement, cannot but have far-reaching consequences not only for the internal politics of those countries, but also for the neighboring countries of central and eastern Europe, and, at some stage, for the United States as well, since we cannot now know what kind political pressures may eventually be brought to bear on those countries' governments relative to the character and future of the Western alliance.

———————

Mr. ROHRABACHER. This has been more philosophical than I expected, but that is fine.

I wonder, Mr. Lewis, do you think that Merkel reads Aristotle? Is that part of what the decisionmaking process, or do you think people there are just trying to cope with a crisis of the moment?

Mr. LEWIS. I don't know much more about the chancellor's thinking than I read in the newspapers. And my impression is that she is coping with a very difficult and stressful situation. But I think it is becoming clear that the strains that are resulting from this are going to have political consequences for her, but are already having consequences for other countries. So I don't know on what basis she is making these decisions, but I think it is probably very improvisational.

Mr. ROHRABACHER. Dr. Shiffman, do you see this influx, and it was interesting you went down to an analysis of when violence happens, and when you put these factors together that we now see as the new reality in Europe, is by your analysis, is that then going to be—that will result in violence one way or the other in the months and years to come?

Mr. SHIFFMAN. Mr. Chairman, I hope not. First, let me say this is the most esoteric congressional hearing probably in a long time. So I appreciate the committee taking on these sort of more philosophical ideas.

The idea that Professor Lewis was talking about and how that merges with what I am talking about is, you know, these ideas that create cohesion among the society are important, and this is what allows for the provision of public goods and peace and stability. And all of that is absolutely at risk right now. You are absolutely right, as you said in your opening statement.

What I tried to point to in my comments are, well, you know, if you are not able to stem the flow, then what are the things that we need to think about? And we need to think about this idea of social isolation and political relevance. That is what sort of the economic literature would suggest. What that means is, and if you look at some of the examples that I cited, you have got this group that doesn't integrate, that is seen as outsiders, they are seen as others, they are not us; they are them, but they might be in sort of in my country now, and there might be some detriment to me from them being here. And that is a great opportunity for what I would call entrepreneur as a violence, to step forward and talk about, you know, recruitment and inciting things that we don't want to see. So those are the things I would point to.

Mr. ROHRABACHER. Well, we did see, here in our own country, where we had some people, young men, who immigrated from Chechnya and leaving their roots behind to come here to live in a freer and more benevolent society and ended up committing a brutal act of terrorism and murdering some of our fellow citizens.

In terms of prefacing your remarks, stemming the flow, I, just for the record, I think that Hungary was totally justified in what it is doing to try to stem the flow. And, frankly, if our European allies are not willing to stem the flow of large numbers of people who are not native to their territory, they will lose their territory.

And let me note, I believe that is true of the United States as well. And we can be proud that we bring in 1 million people, immigrants, into our country every year, more than every other country of the world combined in terms of legal immigration, but we are making sure that—as you noted in your testimony, that we have a screening process, and we are bringing people in who then can be enculturated and assimilated into our society. That is, according to your testimony will, I will say, minimize the chance of some kind of damage.

Mr. SHIFFMAN. That is right.

Mr. ROHRABACHER. I don't think that is possible in Europe. Do you have a comment on what is going on there now in relationship—are these going to be on assimilated populations which will then lead to violence? I will turn to both of you.

Mr. SHIFFMAN. I don't want to comment on the specifics of, you know, any particular European country and what they are doing, but I think from the reading of the newspapers, absolutely, this is something that we need to be concerned about, and that is why I am flagging it in my testimony for you all, is to the extent that the flow is too fast, and you can't do proper screening and vetting, that is the first threat factor, which is sort of the terrorist integrating within the flow.

And then the second is, even when they enter, they are not ISIS affiliated once the threat from radicalization. And that is where I point to those two ideas of socially isolated and politically relevant. And that is something, if we can't slow it down—well, I mean we have to worry about whether we slow it down or not, but those are the things that I suggest the committee think about as they hear further testimony from other folks more expert on the specific policies of the European Union.

Mr. ROHRABACHER. Would you like to comment on that, Dr. Lewis?

Mr. LEWIS. I would simply underline points that both of us have mentioned about the importance of assimilation and the problem, in the particular case we are talking about here, is the numbers of people in the short period of time in which they are coming in. They are talking about possibly of as many as 1½ million refugees into Germany just this year, and I think one has to remember that is on top of millions of refugees that have come in in the last 5, 6, 7 years. Germany is a country of 80 million people, so you can do the math; at a certain point, the percentage creeps up, and the question of the ability to assimilate those immigrants is crucial. The United States is a much larger country. And historically, I think we have done a much better job of assimilating immigrants than the European countries have.

Mr. ROHRABACHER. Well, we, of course, have a culture that is a multi—we accept everybody in. That is what our culture is all about, is being proud of the individual rights that people have in terms of their own backgrounds. So that is not necessarily what keeps the European cultures together, their belief in—our belief in liberty and our belief in human rights, are supposed to be something that units us as Americans. In other areas, they have cultural elements that unit them as a people, a particular religion and some particular customs that they have.

I think that Europe, frankly, this massive influx is going to be, as I mentioned in my opening statement, I believe is going to change the very nature of Europe. And we have seen an historic event, and I believe based on the fact that people are not courageous enough to control their own borders will soon lose their country. There will be some other people there, and people who will have different values and different cultures, and that could happen in the United States as well.

With that said, Mr. Sires, would you like to have your time?

Would you like to use my microphone here?

Mr. SIRES. Absolutely.

Mr. ROHRABACHER. There you go.

Mr. SIRES. Thank you.

Well, having been a refugee myself at the age of 11 and coming to this country, I can tell you from experience that I think the assimilation process in this country has a way of absorbing you and making you part of this country. And if you talk to my brother and my younger brother, who was born here, I mean, they have very little remnants of what it was to grow up in Cuba like I did. I came over when I was 11 years old.

My concern, I mean, is that these countries do not have the welcoming that this country has for these refugees. And I understand that, because these are not large countries. And if you have an influx of people, very different from your culture, they stand to congregate and basically stand apart from the rest of the country, which I think eventually is going to hurt those countries. Because they will want to keep their own culture. They do not want to be part of the country that they are in. I don't know. This country here is very different. You want to be part of this country, at least that was in my family.

And I can see where Hungary would want to close its borders. It is not a large country. They don't have the resources. I can see for some of the other countries closing their borders. It is a very different situation that we have here.

Now, Germany needs workers, but I think even now they are starting to rethink the amount of people that they need and the amount of people they are going to accept.

And, you know, my question is, which of the countries have been most impacted—what countries have been most impacted by this influx of refugees? Dr. Shiffman?

Mr. SHIFFMAN. So let me address your first point, Congressman, which is there is—putting this back into economic terms, right, there is a tradeoff. Everything is a tradeoff. And, you know, in the United States, we have the melting pot, the phrase I used in my testimony. We have this identity of we are the melting pot. We have hyphenated Americans, and that is fine. Right? I am a Cuban-American, a Russian-American, a whatever-American, and that is welcoming here. And that is a wonderful thing. And that has led to what makes us great, as the chairman said, and that also contributes to economic growth and development and GDP growth and trade and all of these other things.

There is a tradeoff that European States have to make right now, which is, they need the workers, but that is going to—they can get workers, and they can get GDP growth; they can get economic growth at the cost of that melting pot. Right? And are the European States really ready for a melting pot approach? Do they want hyphenated, you know, fill in the blank, or do they want to keep their national identity? That is the nature of the tradeoff right now.

My third point is that there is an economic opportunity here. Right? There is an opportunity for increasing GDP growth, but it is going to cost you culturally. It is going to cost you ethnically and nationally, and that may not be what people are willing to do. And I don't think they are. And if that is the case, then, you know, the rest of my testimony was, well, how do we address what really might backfire on us, which is, where is the violence going to come from. And that is what I think we need to focus on.

Mr. SIRES. And I think the influx has been so quickly, so many, that the security issue is very important.

Mr. SHIFFMAN. Right.

Mr. SIRES. I remember as a boy when my father was taken away when we first arrived for about 4 or 5 days. And they went through—my father went through a whole process, did you participate in the communist party? Were you involved in the communist party back then. And then after, you know, after the 4 or 5 days, he was returned to us.

I don't think these countries have any way of screening the people that are going through there like what we went through when I first arrived here.

So to me, I agree with the notion that these countries could be taking in some people that are going to basically try to disrupt our country or disrupt Europe. And for those countries, it is very difficult to keep letting people in the countries who are not screened like they were.

Mr. SHIFFMAN. So my quick response, in the U.S., the reason we build walls on our border is to slow the flow and to direct the flow where we can screen people. That is why we have walls on the U.S. borders. If you look at high-density urban populations without a wall, people are run across the U.S.-Mexican border and within 60 seconds they are in a safe house. We put a wall up, slows them down, so they have to get through the deserts of Arizona or they have to go through a point of entry. So walls make sense when it comes to securing borders. That is a good thing.

And so when we see it applied in Europe, it is the same idea. The broader point I tried to make in my testimony also is, this isn't a Texas problem. This is a U.S. problem. So when we think about Europe, we need to think about how do we stem the flow? How do we slow it down? How do we get control of it? How do we do screening in a way that it is not just Hungary's problem, but it is something that is collectively addressed both in the costs and the benefits side.

Mr. SIRES. The other aspect of this is that I think people who come here eventually want to become American citizens and participate in the process. I know my grandmother was 83 years old when she first became a citizen so she can vote for her grandson. You know, she never learned the language.

Mr. POE. Did she vote for you?

Mr. SIRES. Absolutely. More than once.

But, you know, it was a process. And no matter how much you try to teach her English or everything, she would never learn it.

And my mother used to say that if she ever lost this finger in this country, she be a mute. Because she used to go to the store and say one, one, that is how she bought things. But, you know, you assimilate. And this country has a way of just taking you in.

I don't think these countries have that capacity, and I don't know if the people—and we want it to be assimilated, quite frankly. And those people that are going to those countries, I don't know if they want to be assimilated. Would you agree with that, Dr. Lewis?

Mr. LEWIS. Yes. I think that is a real question at the moment. I mean, there are two important things here I would mention. One is that the influx of refugees, which is quite heavy here at the moment, comes in combination with the demographic problems, the loss of growth, the natural fertility in most Western European countries, well below replacement, and that is why they need workers from the outside. But what is crucial is to have an orderly process of immigration.

My wife's grandparents came over here from Italy, and her father, who grew up here with those parents became a decorated veteran of World War II, loved the United States. He learned that being here, acquired those sentiments of attachment to the country and willingness to sacrifice for it. That takes time, and it requires a kind of orderly process, and that is what is not there.

Mr. SIRES. That is not there. The absorption in those countries is not there either like it is here. You know, for some reason, you know, we drink espresso, but then we like coffee, too.

Thank you, Mr. Chairman.

Mr. ROHRABACHER. All right. Let's just note that Cuban-Americans have done pretty well, and they have done so well in assimilating that I predict that there will be a Cuban-American that is President of the United States, but I won't tell you which one.

And let me also just note here, when we were talking about the assimilation of people in the United States in the last 50 years during the Cold War. I mentioned the Hungarian uprising. The people who came here during the Cold War, and there were many, many people who were escaping communism came here. They came here and helped us to thwart this evil theory of communism that threatened world peace. Their assimilation helped us, as Americans, understand when our neighbors saying oh, my gosh, they won't even let people worship God the way they want in communist countries, that alerted the American people to a threat.

Unfortunately, what it appears, that many of the people who are arriving here from the Middle East, who are Islamic, are not here as enemies of the radical Islam that drove them here. And, in fact, just the opposite. Sometimes you have people who come here and expect that they are going to have their women covered up. And quite frankly, I think that is an insult to our values as a people, and not to mention people who come here from Islamic countries who think they can still have honor killings and things such as this.

That's not assimilation, and that is a threat to—and on top of it, unlike the Cubans, who came here, who are enemies of communism, these people aren't necessarily enemies—well they are not enemies at all of Islam. And I am not saying people of Islam is the enemy, but certainly radical Islam is. And anybody who comes here should be part of the team. And I could say, Cuban-Americans, we are proud of you guys. I mean, Cuban-Americans have do so much for our country as so many of our immigrants that are coming from elsewhere, like your father from—your father-in-law from Italy and such.

And I will leave that with Judge Poe, who has got some insights for us as well.

Mr. POE. Thank you, Mr. Chairman. And thank you, all, for being here.

Professor Lewis, I am intrigued that you study and teach natural law. I didn't know anybody did that in the country anymore. I am a great fan of natural law and the history, especially of the founding of our country under the theory of natural law.

I have been to Turkey, and I have seen the refugee camps. The one I was in had about 180,000 people from Syria. And this problem is increasing because, of course, of the situation that we are all aware of in Syria where you have got Assad, you have got rebels, a mixed bag of a bunch of folks, we don't know who they all are, and then we have ISIS all in there trying to control it, and the Russians come in trying to make a power struggle, and everybody's running for the hills.

The people coming into Europe, we don't know who they all are, because we don't know who they are. And it seems to me that they are everybody. They are those genuine refugees that are running for their lives because of Assad or ISIS. They are people looking for economic opportunities. They are people who are coming into Europe maybe to cause mischief, but various reasons. And if I understand what has been reported about their migration, the goal seems to be for a large amount of them to go into Europe, Eastern Europe, move into Germany and then even move up into the Nordic State. And there is no end in sight until we run out of people.

I read some estimates that there are going to be 5 million folks moving into Europe. I don't know if that is true or not, but it is a lot of folks coming in. There is no unified plan on what to do with all those people or who is going to pay for it.

One of the, I think, issues of any nation is to protect its sovereignty or its integrity, however you want to define that. But part of that is knowing who comes into their country and deciding whether they can stay or not. But the main thing, know who they are, identify them. And early on, it looked like people were just coming in into Europe and going wherever they can get and never did know who they were.

I think countries like the border European Union countries, specifically like Hungary, not only have a right but an obligation to find out who is coming into their country. For the U.S. to second-guess them and belittle them, and our soap opera Ambassador dressing them down last week, I thought that was a big mistake. Because, if I understand the way the system works, if a country identifies someone at their border as a refugee, and the person keeps moving, let's say to Germany, gets to Germany, Germany may have the ability, authority to send them back to the original border entry country.

Is that your understanding, either one of you all? Under the current agreement in the European Union? Do either one of you know?

Mr. LEWIS. The current rules, the Dublin rules, I think, have been largely dispensed with. I think those were the rules, but I think there really aren't many rules at the moment——

Mr. POE. So we don't have any—we don't know what could happen to the migrant that gets all the way to Germany or to France or Sweden and that country decides, you are not staying here. They go back to where they came from or the original entry country. That seems to me to promote just chaos in Europe.

Europe is, what, 500 million; United States is 360 million or so. And you have lots of people coming in. It would just seem to me that nations would have the authority to identify and track and find out who is coming in. And then as my friend from New York pointed out, what is the purpose of folks coming in? Are they coming in to assimilate into whatever country, or are they coming in to form another culture in the country? I think France has found that they have had this problem with assimilation of people who come to their country.

So I guess my question is, what should the United States be doing? And we are observing and criticizing, but what should we be doing about this migration issue in Europe?

Mr. SHIFFMAN. So, Judge Poe, I agree with the way you have laid it out very nicely. The direct concern to the United States is so, to the extent this happens and these folks' mass migrations happen into Europe, they are now in visa waiver countries, and so they now come into the United States. So this very quickly becomes a United States, you know, national security issue. So we absolutely have an interest in this immediately.

My comments about the way Europe could handle this better is to look at some of the things that we have learned here. First of all, the border states aren't solely responsible for this. Right?

Mr. POE. You mean financially?

Mr. SHIFFMAN. Financially. Fiscally. Right? You know, looking at the border states——

Mr. POE. And right now, is it your understanding that the border—every country is kind of on their own as far as paying for the migrants that are there?

Mr. SHIFFMAN. Again, with the caveat I am not an EU follower, that is my understanding that the burden is falling disproportionately on the border states for doing that screening, which makes absolutely no sense for U.S. national security, let alone for Europe's national security.

As you said, we need to, to use your phrase, which I like, we have to know first and foremost who it is, and second, why they are coming. We are not built to do that right now in Europe, and it seems what the United States needs to do is be a part of fixing that. Right? This is——

Mr. POE. I am going to send you over there with your expertise in ICE and border security.

Mr. SHIFFMAN. Well, you know, the United States Government knows an awful lot about border security. I was fortunate enough to be a part of the early days of DHS here. Lots of folks have experience that could be beneficial to the European Union. I think they need to address it as the European Union, though. This isn't Hungary's problem; this is EU's problem, and by extension the United States as well.

Mr. POE. I am about out of time, professor. In fact, I am. Do you want to weigh in on that?

Mr. LEWIS. Well, you know, the statement that I prepared, submitted ahead of time, one element of it is, that it is an absolute first responsibility of national governments to protect the common good of the people of those countries, to secure the rule of law and the protection of the fundamental rights of those people, and they have that. It is a very solemn obligation for the governing authority of any country. And now there is a natural tendency and a correct tendency to want to be generous and hospitable to immigrants; there are compelling humanitarian reasons for that. And I think, you know, the Germans have tried to do that, maybe overtried in some ways.

But it has to be understood that the first responsibility of governments is to protect the security of their people. And some of these issues really, really could have an impact there. In just yesterday's Wall Street Journal, there was a story about forged passports and the market in forged passports, people coming into Europe now, usually what they do is apparently throw the passports away once they get to the country of destination, and then they are equipped with a whole new set of identity documents, which could then be used to travel to other places as well. There may be no way of knowing where they originally came from or what their intentions are. And it is a matter of internal security, a justified function of government to police that.

Mr. POE. Thank you, Mr. Chairman.

Mr. ROHRABACHER. Ms. Frankel.

Ms. FRANKEL. Thank you, very much. Well, you know, we could talk about border security and sovereign rights all day. But here is the cruel fact of it all: We are dealing with the worst humanitarian crisis in, what, since World War II. And these people, they have to go somewhere, because they are getting killed and tortured, and they are starving. It is a horrible situation.

First question I would like you to comment—you know, answer, if you want to weigh in, which I think is important for our public to understand, and that is—because we are looking at all this afar, and I think we can understand the humanitarian part of this. I would like your opinion on what is happening now in Europe, how that would affect our own economic or national security here in the United States? What are the long-term implications?

Mr. SHIFFMAN. So, first, let me agree that this is—it is hard not to think of this first and foremost as a humanitarian crisis that we all have to take very seriously. And I think—for myself, that was my first response, is well, as a national security professional, you are still sort of—the humanitarian component of this still comes first to mind.

So, in my testimony, as I suggested, Ms. Frankel, there may be ways—if you are not going to let everybody in, and as Judge Poe said, not everybody is coming for the same reasons. Right? Not everybody is coming in because they are persecuted and fleeing for their lives. They see an opportunity to get into Europe, get into Northern Europe and get into a nice welfare State.

Ms. FRANKEL. Right.

Mr. SHIFFMAN. So if we can screen out, which is hard to do, if we can screen out, then it makes sense to me to focus on the most vulnerable populations first, and that is something I think we know how to do. At least the United States knows how to do that.

Ms. FRANKEL. Okay. Well, thank you for saying what you said. Maybe my question wasn't clear. I think it is important for our public here in the United States to understand that there are economic consequences and potential national security consequences if we ignore what is going on in Europe and in Syria and in other parts of the region that are affected by these refugees. I thought maybe you could comment on that?

Mr. SHIFFMAN. Sure. As I pointed out in my testimony, what concerns me is having unintegrated populations that have political relevance, and that is what I think historically, when we look back, tends to provide the opportunity for violence, definitely and stability.

So as Professor Lewis said, right, these shared—the common good, the shared stories, the shared languages, these are always in which we integrate populations, as Mr. Sires said, we failed to do that. If they come in anyway, large numbers——

Ms. FRANKEL. All right. I don't mean to interrupt you, but maybe this is just not in your area of expertise. That is not a criticism, all right. I mean, I think there are economic consequences and security consequences if we ignore what is going on, but not because we are afraid of terrorists coming in. I mean, quite frankly, I think most of the people who are being—that are fleeing Syria are innocent people who are good, decent people, and they are not going to threaten our lives. I think the bigger threat is we do nothing.

So I will go to another subject then, all right. Which is—and I think maybe Mr. Poe started to get into this with you, but do you think that the United States should give more financial aid toward the refugees that are now going into Europe? Because I know we are doing it in Syria; we are doing it in Lebanon. I mean, the displaced refugees in Syria and Lebanon and Jordan and Turkey. Do you have an opinion as to whether or not we should increase our efforts in Europe?

Mr. SHIFFMAN. No, ma'am. I don't know how much we are giving, and if it is——

Ms. FRANKEL. Okay. So that is outside your——

Mr. SHIFFMAN. That is outside my——

Ms. FRANKEL. And I guess our philosopher over here, you just— no comment?

Mr. LEWIS. No. I mean, the United States is a generous country, and I hope it continues to be generous, but as far as exactly how much money is available for what, I just don't know.

Ms. FRANKEL. Okay. All right. You know what, but I did enjoy your testimony.

And I think I will yield back, Mr. Chair.

Mr. ROHRABACHER. All right. Thank you very much.

Mr. Weber.

Mr. WEBER. Dr. Lewis, you said in your prepared remarks, and I am paraphrasing, that private property doesn't belong to anyone. Would you go back through that for me, please?

Mr. LEWIS. Yeah. What I was talking about there was the resources that people need to live, the most important ones, come initially just from the earth itself. And my point was at the beginning, if we sort of mentally put ourselves back, you might say, just hypothetically at the beginning of the world, no particular piece of the earth belongs to any particular person naturally.

Mr. WEBER. And yet you recognize——

Mr. LEWIS. We acquire things.

Mr. WEBER. You recognize from Biblical days that there was properties bought and sold, for example. So some time back thousands of years ago, that process began.

Mr. LEWIS. Because of facts about human nature, the fact that we tend to take care of things more effectively when we own them and——

Mr. WEBER. Right.

Mr. LEWIS [continuing]. People quarrel over things, it makes sense——

Mr. WEBER. And that is where——

Mr. LEWIS [continuing]. That we parcel out.

Mr. WEBER. Well, that is where I was going to go, I mean, because ownership, actually, you know, I would submit makes people be better stewards of their property.

Mr. LEWIS. Absolutely. But I was making an analogy to territory itself, that particular governments are better stewards of their territory and of the order of their territory than having no particular governments and borders and so forth.

Mr. WEBER. So in your estimation, is Hungary being a good steward of their borders?

Mr. LEWIS. From what I can tell, Hungary is doing what they think is necessary to protect their national security.

Mr. WEBER. That is what I want to hear, especially with our Ambassador sitting here.

Dr. Shiffman, you said that opportunity for economic growth for all of these refugees or immigrants coming in, but don't you think that perhaps it is going to be an overburdening on the infrastructure? I mean, you talked about an opportunity for economic growth. Is there no down side that you see? I am talking about economically now.

Mr. SHIFFMAN. Yeah. Right. In terms of sort of just per capita and GDP growth, it most certainly is a net benefit, but it might not be a benefit for everybody. So there will—I will give you an example. And we face this in the United States with having open borders and free trade and stuff like that. So there are certainly individuals who will lose out on an economic opportunity as other people come in and replace them and——

Mr. WEBER. Is there a timeframe involved? I mean, they are not going to get that economic benefit in the first 6 months or a year, right? They are going to be really overburdened for a while?

Mr. SHIFFMAN. So what I would do is go back to the points we have been talking about, is knowing who is crossing the border. I imagine there are some folks who are highly trained, highly educated who will be able to contribute to the economy right away. There might be other folks who, you know, it might take a generation.

Mr. WEBER. Well, let me address part of that open borders. You mentioned the United States actually shares—has the responsibility of—I come from Texas.

Mr. SHIFFMAN. Yes, sir.

Mr. WEBER. I was in the Texas legislature, and my second term I was the vice-chair of the Borders Committee, and I can tell you things about our southern border. Of the 2,000 miles the United States has with Mexico, Texas has about 1,167 miles, almost two-thirds of them, and it would scare you.

The years that I was there, the 4 years I was there, the Texas legislature put $200 million in border security; unfortunately, the United States did not. After I left, they came in and put $400 million the first term I was gone, and the last term they put over $500 million in. So I want to make that plug for not only the great state of Texas, but to point out the country of the United States is not really shouldering up under the responsibility of securing our southern border. Okay.

It is interesting to me, and I am trying to read my notes while I am talking, one of you said that maybe the European Union ought to shoulder up under that burden and pony up some money. Was that you, Dr.—was it you?

Okay. How do you expect to make that happen if we can't get the United States to do that?

Mr. SHIFFMAN. I don't intend to make it happen. I am just suggesting to the committee some things that you might want to take up in your conversations.

Mr. WEBER. That is a battle that we might not be able to win.

Mr. SHIFFMAN. I understand.

Mr. WEBER. And then, let's see. Dr. Shiffman, you also said in your discourse with Congresswoman Frankel that the humanitarian component of the crisis has to come up first, but at what point—you were talking about—she was talking about people being taken in, you know, that they were—I mean, I am not going to put words in Lois's mouth, but I think she said they were all pretty friendly and nice, most of them, you know, insinuating that we ought to be willing to take some of them in was, I guess, where she was going with that.

But at what point does the humanitarian concept of our citizens take precedence because of the danger? Would you speak to that?

Mr. SHIFFMAN. Sure. The precedence of our citizenship should—our citizens come first.

Mr. WEBER. Should be first and foremost.

Mr. SHIFFMAN. First and foremost, yes, sir.

Mr. WEBER. Okay. How do you balance those two?

Mr. SHIFFMAN. Through this political process that we are taking part in here.

Mr. WEBER. Okay. Are you aware of about 3:20 today, CNN is reporting that the United States intelligence are saying that they believe a bomb brought the airliner down in Egypt, a bomb onboard the plane? So when you talk about people coming over and either assimilating into their—you, know, there was—I don't remember which one said that there was a problem that maybe terrorists were being embedded in the refugee stream, or that once they got there, they would radicalize others in the nation.

Well, I think what we are seeing is the effect of some radicalization, some terrorism right now. Do you know how many men and women and children lost their lives on that airliner? It is about 230 something, wasn't it?

So I am just struggling with the idea that somehow we have to focus on the humanitarian crisis to the exclusion of our own citizens' safety. That is just a huge concern to me.

Mr. Chairman, I will yield back.

Mr. ROHRABACHER. Thank you very much. Just a few thoughts—and, Mr. Sires, do you have a 1-minute or so, 2-minute closing statement?

Mr. SIRES. Well, I just wanted——

Mr. ROHRABACHER. Use this microphone.

Mr. SIRES. I just wanted to thank you. And I am still very concerned about the long-term impact of the constant refugee flow into Europe. I think it is going to disrupt some of these countries, because they just don't have the money or the ability to take in this population.

So I think we have to just keep an eye on this situation, because eventually we are going to have to make sure that the security of this country comes first.

Mr. ROHRABACHER. Well, thank you very much. Thank you for the witnesses.

And just a few thoughts, that the massive influx and out-of-control influx that we see in Europe is not simply a European phenomena, although I believe that one of the factors that we have to look at, historic factors in Europe, that Europe lost tens of millions of young men in World War I and World War II. And during that time period, those young men disappeared from the population equation, thus, the children of the people who were prevented from having children because they died at a younger age, and their children don't exist.

And you go right down how many people exist, Europe would probably have many more, maybe hundreds of millions, maybe 100 million more people had those people killed in these vicious wars not been eliminated from the equation. And thus, we see a Europe that is underpopulated now from what it would have been except for war. During that time period, there wasn't a massive war of extermination going on in the Middle East, and in the Muslim parts of the world.

That is bound to—you also see the effect of abortion on Europe. Abortion has been a major factor in limiting the population in Europe. And, again, the babies that have been aborted in the last 50 years don't have children who don't have children, and thus you have a shrinkage of population going on. With that, we face a population where we have people who were having families of six and seven and eight people. And when you have societies juxtaposed like that, you are going to have—it is going to have an impact, and we are seeing it now.

And so with that said, that massive influx, however, should not be looked at as only a possible European situation. In the United States, I believe this influx was started when Merkel decided that she would then change the policy, and anybody who could get to Germany, they were going to take them in. Well, when that word went out, all of a sudden trying to stop the flow of immigrants illegally into Europe became untenable. That is the same dynamic at play in the United States.

When the people, the poor people of the world figure out that they can come here, and once they get here, they are going to be able to get a job, they are going to be able to get government benefits just like everybody else, there will be the out of control massive inflow that Europe has had right now, to the point that it might change or undermine the basic cultural elements that unite all of us. And that is a great threat.

We should be taking a lesson here, because whether it is—and I am not just talking about—most people—unfortunately, the immigration debate has been focused on Mexico, and this is not a Mexican problem. This is an idea that once the word goes out to the world, we have a major illegal immigration from China now and in Asia, we also have people from all over Latin America. And if we put out the same message that Merkel put out for her country, we will have the same out of control influx into our society, and we are on the edge of that right now. So let us learn the lesson of Europe.

Thank you for joining us and giving us your insights, both philosophically and practically. And with that said, this hearing—one moment. I am going to announce one thing. At the close of the hearing, I thought I would announce tomorrow I will be submitting a piece of legislation that suggests that those people in Middle Eastern countries that are now suffering from radical Islamic terrorism, those countries in which Christians have been targeted for genocide, that when it comes to immigration and refugee status, that those Christians, who are targeted for genocide, will have priority over other people in trying to find refuge in the United States. I will be dropping that bill tomorrow.

Thank you very much. This hearing is adjourned.

[Whereupon, at 4:13 p.m., the subcommittee was adjourned.]

APPENDIX

MATERIAL SUBMITTED FOR THE RECORD

SUBCOMMITTEE HEARING NOTICE
COMMITTEE ON FOREIGN AFFAIRS
U.S. HOUSE OF REPRESENTATIVES
WASHINGTON, D.C. 20515-6128

Subcommittee on Europe, Eurasia, and Emerging Threats
Dana Rohrabacher (R-CA), Chairman

October 28, 2015

TO: MEMBERS OF THE COMMITTEE ON FOREIGN AFFAIRS

You are respectfully requested to attend an OPEN hearing of the Committee on Foreign Affairs, to be held by the Subcommittee on Europe, Eurasia, and Emerging Threats in Room 2200 of the Rayburn House Office Building (and available on the Committee website at http://www.ForeignAffairs.house.gov):

DATE: Wednesday, November 4, 2015

TIME: 2:00 p.m.

SUBJECT: Challenge to Europe: The Growing Refugee Crisis

WITNESSES: Gary Shiffman, Ph.D
                    Adjunct Professor
                    Center for Security Studies
                    Georgetown University

                    V. Bradley Lewis, Ph.D.
                    Associate Professor
                    School of Philosophy
                    The Catholic University of America

By Direction of the Chairman

The Committee on Foreign Affairs seeks to make its facilities accessible to persons with disabilities. If you are in need of special accommodations, please call 202/225-5021 at least four business days in advance of the event, whenever practicable. Questions with regard to special accommodations in general (including availability of Committee materials in alternative formats and assistive listening devices) may be directed to the Committee.

COMMITTEE ON FOREIGN AFFAIRS

MINUTES OF SUBCOMMITTEE ON _____*Europe, Eurasia, and Emerging Thretas*_____ HEARING

Day___*Wednesday*___Date___*November 4, 2015*___Room____*2200 Rayburn*____

Starting Time ____*3:00 pm*___Ending Time ___*4:13 pm*___

Recesses |_____| (____to ____) (____to ____) (____to ____) (____to ____) (____to ____) (____to ____)

Presiding Member(s)

Rep. Rohrabacher

Check all of the following that apply:

Open Session ✓   Electronically Recorded (taped) ✓
Executive (closed) Session ☐   Stenographic Record ✓
Televised ☐

TITLE OF HEARING:

Challenge to Europe: The Growing Refugee Crisis

SUBCOMMITTEE MEMBERS PRESENT:

Rep. Poe, Rep. Weber, Rep. Sires, Rep. Frankel

NON-SUBCOMMITTEE MEMBERS PRESENT: *(Mark with an * if they are not members of full committee.)*

N/A

HEARING WITNESSES: Same as meeting notice attached? Yes ✓ No ☐
(If "no", please list below and include title, agency, department, or organization.)

STATEMENTS FOR THE RECORD: *(List any statements submitted for the record.)*

TIME SCHEDULED TO RECONVENE _____
or
TIME ADJOURNED _*4:13 pm*_

Subcommittee Staff Director